The Ladies of Miller's

By the same author

Remarkably Sad and Mysterious Circumstances

Dale House Press
Lewes
1996

Half-hour play for radio dramatising the death of
Douglas Byng-Stamper which occurred when the
family was living at Northease Manor.

Cedric Morris *The Sisters* 1935

The
Ladies of Miller's

*

by

Diana Crook

Diana Crook

*

Dale House Press
Lewes

Diana Crook
The Ladies of Miller's
Copyright © 1996
by Diana Crook

ISBN 1 900841 01 0

This book was designed
at the Dale House Press.
The text is printed in 10pt Palatino
using an Apple Macintosh computer
and LaserWriter.

Dale House Press
Lewes
November 1996

For
Lucy, Anna and Victoria

※

※

Acknowledgements

It was in 1978 that I moved with my family into a house in Lewes High Street, East Sussex. I heard talk of the eccentric old ladies who had lived there some years before and was intrigued to find lithography stones in the garden, one still bearing a faint design and the initials D G. It was not until the publication of Frances Spalding's biography of Vanessa Bell in 1983, however, that I realised just how remarkable and influential they had been. All traces of their lives and works seemed to have disappeared. I spent many years of often frustrating research to try and discover as much as I could about them. The people of Lewes hospitably opened their homes to me and told wonderful stories of the ladies, many of them contradictory. Eventually I had enough material to write a number of articles and later in 1989 to help with the arrangement of a six-week exhibition, 'The Ladies of Miller's', at the Towner Gallery, Eastbourne.

My husband having recently set up a private press in our present home, we were able, with the help of Lewes District Council, to produce a hand-made private press edition of fifty copies. It is pleasing to report that demand has led to this first trade edition.

I would like to thank Professor Quentin Bell for permission to quote from the letters of Clive Bell; Stephen and Roger Musgrave for permission to quote from the unpublished autobiography 'I Ought Not To Have Done It' by Clifford Musgrave; Dr James Andrews for permission to quote from 'A Tour Into Sussex' from *The Torrington Diaries*, and Michael Chase of The Cedric Morris Estate for permission to reproduce the portrait of the ladies, *The Sisters*.

Very many people have been most generous in their assistance with my researches and it is impossible to mention them all. Especial thanks are, however, due to the following:-

Mr A F L Adams, Barbican Museum, Professor Quentin Bell, Jim Bartholomew, Colin Brent, Lord Briggs of Lewes, East Sussex Records Office, Diana Gardner, Angelica Garnett, Henrietta Garnett, Mr C S Geering, Mrs E M Greenwood, Peggy Heriot, William Inman, Mrs V B Lamb, Betty Lewis, Mrs Lindsay Smith, The Listener, Gladys Morris, Trekkie Parsons, Frances Partridge, Margaret Musgrave, The New Statesman, Mr B B Pratt, Julia Ramos, The Redfern Gallery (Gordon Samuel), Richard Shone, Frances Spalding, Simon and Julian Target, The Tate Gallery (Richard Morphet), Mary Teakle, Ivy Thain, The Towner Gallery (Penny Johnson), Miss K Vinall, Joan Warburton, Ivor Wycherley, Monica Yonge.

Many years have passed since my work began and I am sadly aware that several of the above are no longer alive. I am only sorry that they cannot read this book to which they made such an invaluable contribution.

Diana Crook
November 1996

✳

Introduction

Shortly after the outbreak of war, two genteel sisters of independent means and odd aspect purchased a Georgian-fronted house in Lewes High Street and converted the stables in the back garden into a small well-lit gallery. In July 1941 Miller's Gallery was opened to promote the arts at a time when virtually all opportunities for their appreciation had ceased. In The New Statesman of that month, Clive Bell wrote: 'The gallery is called Miller's because the house of which it was once the stable is so-called and the house is called Miller's because it belonged to a miller: they are as simple as that in Sussex.' At the same time he wrote from Charleston to his friend Frances Partridge at Ham Spray: 'Then on Saturday there was the opening of Miller's - the new little gallery at Lewes from which is to emanate a revival of all the arts in Sussex - a new regionalism. I have said so myself in the preface, and Mrs Byng-Stamper will see to it. It was a fine affair with about 200 people in a hole much smaller than the black one at Calcutta.'

The ladies' aim was to create the first centre of regional art in the country. During the next 4 years over 50 exhibitions, lectures and recitals of the first order were put on for enthusiastic art-lovers. Later, after the war, the sisters went on the revitalise the art of lithography and to influence British painters to experiment with printing. What made these women, nearing sixty, embark on such an enterprising and unusual venture? The answer lies many years earlier in a tragedy of still unexplained circumstances.

✳

The Early Years

Frances Byng-Stamper and her sister Caroline Lucas (Bay and Mouie to their friends) were born in 1882 and 1886 respectively. They were the younger daughters of Charles Lucas, a member of one of the old county families of Ireland. When a midshipman on the HMS Hecla during the engagement of Bomersund during the Crimean War, he saved the ship by running forward to pick up a live shell that had landed on deck with its fuse spluttering, and threw it overboard. It exploded as it hit the water. This act of bravery inspired Queen Victoria to create the order of the Victoria Cross to be awarded for acts of outstanding gallantry and made Lucas, at 18 years old, its first recipient. He was decorated by the Queen at an inauguration ceremony in Hyde Park in 1857. His act of heroism caught the imagination of the nation and was illustrated in Punch magazine, in popular prints and even on tins of tea and biscuits. It was when Lucas reached his mid-forties that his old commander from the HMS Hecla, now Admiral Sir William Hutcheon Hall, summoned him to his death bed and made an extraordinary request. He begged Lucas to take care of his wife Hilare and to marry his only daughter Frances. Lucas, an incurable romantic, agreed. The marriage was not a success for Frances was arrogant and violent-tempered and far too aware of her position as a member of the Byng family, being grand-daughter to the 6th Viscount Torrington. To her younger daughters she gave the second name of Byng as a reminder of their aristocratic inheritance. It was something that the sisters were never able to forget. Throughout their lives they assumed they occupied a superior station in life which entitled them to be arrogant to the lower orders. To those, however, whom they considered possessed good breeding or outstanding artistic talents, they were charming, attentive and beautifully mannered.

Though the ladies would have been the last to acknowledge the fact, George Byng, the founder of the noble Kentish family, was the son of a draper. He had a spectacular naval career rapidly reaching the rank of Admiral. An ardent supporter of William III, he captured Gibraltar in the war of the Spanish succession, defeated the fleet of the Old Pretender off Scotland and crowned his career by destroying the Spanish Fleet at Messina. He was knighted by a grateful Queen Anne in 1704 and created 1st Viscount Torrington by George I in 1721. His fourth son, John, also entered the navy and owed his rapid promotion to Admiral of the Blue much to his father's influence. In 1756, however, he failed to relieve Menorca from a siege by the French and retreated ignominiously to Gibraltar. He was court martialled, cleared of want of courage but found guilty of an error of judgment. Despite a recommendation of mercy, in March 1757 he was shot by a firing squad at Portsmouth. This somewhat drastic measure prompted Voltaire to remark in *Candide* that the English found it necessary to shoot an admiral from time to time 'pour encourager les autres'. Not surprisingly the sisters would not countenance any allegations of cowardice made against their kinsman and considered he had been made a scapegoat. A poem found among their papers, which makes up in lively indignation for what it lacks in sophistication, echoes their sentiments:-

'... They who had sought to make his name
A shameful dishonoured thing
Could they have met that horrible doom
So bravely as Admiral Byng?

Firm and erect to the Quarter Deck
He walked, like a discrowned king
His face was pale - but no officer there
So calm as Admiral Byng!

Quietly facing the glittering steel,
"Don't cover my eyes!" he said;
But when he heard of the soldiers' fear
He bent his haughty head!

A thought for others, his latest deed
Hark! how the muskets ring!
A flash - a smoke - and a sharp report!
They have *murdered* Admiral Byng!

And a brave Jack Tar, on the gory deck
Shudders, and turns away;
And says aloud that "the noblest blood
In England is shed today!" ...'

Apart from their noble Byng connections the ladies also enjoyed hinting at numerous friends in high places. This prompted the Charleston joke that the ladies had no education because they were mixed up with royalty. One genuine royal connection was Princess Louise, Duchess of Argyll and fourth daughter of Queen Victoria. Before Charles Lucas married, he was living in the Western Highlands with his sister and brother-in-law and had become a close friend of Lord Lorne, later to become the Duke of Argyll. The Lucas's first child, Hilare, was born in Scotland and was later to become the Princess's Lady in Waiting. Although the family then moved away from Scotland to Kent, the three little girls were made 'wards' of the Princess who maintained a keen interest in them and in due course became godmother to Frances's own son. The Princess's later involvement with the three sisters was, however, to be disrupted by a grave split in the Lucas family. Shortly after Charles Lucas's death in 1914, Hilare, a sweet-faced, gentle-natured girl, committed an unforgivable sin in the eyes of her mother and sisters. She married a

Roman Catholic and adopted her husband's faith. The widow of Charles Lucas, a member of the Grand Lodge of Ulster, never forgave her eldest daughter who was cast out from the family and never spoken of again. Her sisters did nothing to heal the breach, even after their mother's death, and the only surviving member of the family, Hilare's son, never heard mention of his aunts.

Frances was the first of the girls to marry. Her husband, Edwin Stamper, while the son of a respectable Pembrokeshire doctor and a Lieutenant in the Royal Welsh Fusiliers, was not considered by her mother to be a gentleman. Even the birth of a grandson and Edwin's promotion to Captain did not reconcile her to the match. After the further shock of Hilare's marriage all her hopes centred on her youngest daughter who pleased her mother by developing her artistic talents and avoided the pitfalls of a matrimonial misalliance by remaining single. Caroline became her darling child to whom she bequeathed all her estate. Caroline, however, was not fond of her mother and lost no time at her death in 1925 in putting her inheritance at the disposal of her sister and brother-in-law. Edwin left the army and with his wife and sister-in-law purchased the Northease Estate near Lewes in order to start a new life as a gentleman farmer.

The estate, once linked to the monastic order at Lewes Priory, consisted of a fine Queen Anne Manor house together with a smaller neighbouring farm, 20 or so cottages and over a thousand acres of land. It lay in a superb position surrounded by the Sussex Downs and

Cedric Morris *The Sisters* 1935 Detail of Frances

looking across the Ouse Valley towards Mount Caburn. The sisters determined to build up the estate into a showpiece for modern farming. Everything was to be of the best with no expense spared. They bought flocks of sturdy Southdown sheep and a herd of pedigree Jersey cattle which they named The Culverden Jersey Herd after their previous Kentish home. The house was expensively reappointed and staffed by a cook, housemaid, parlour maid, kitchen maid, daily cleaner and male secretary. An architect visited once a week to advise on alterations and additions. The most modern of equipment was ordered for the farm - the local milking machines were judged to be inadequate and the very latest models were sent over from Sweden accompanied by a Swedish expert to demonstrate their superiority. The family entertained lavishly. Every week a hamper of gourmet provisions was received from an emporium in Tunbridge Wells and the cellars were hung with pheasants and stocked with fine wines. Breakfasts consisted of hot trays filled with kidneys, kedgeree, grilled bacon and scrambled egg. Tea was served from elegant Queen Anne silver tea-sets. For dinner in the panelled dining room, where ancestral portraits of the Byngs stared down, the ladies always dressed formally, favouring lace and sequins.

Frances ruled the household with a rod of iron, dismissing the cook summarily for daring to take time off to attend the Plumpton Races with her young man. Caroline took little part in the running of the house and glided quietly about the manor, painting for long hours in her bedroom or hunting enthusiastically and aggressively with the local gentry. She was often heard to boast that she could ride five miles in any direction and still be on her own land. She took a keen interest in the Jersey herd (hence reputedly her nickname) and would watch over the cows herself if they were sick. In 1926 an outbreak of foot and mouth threatened the animals. Immediately the farm-hands were ordered to remain within the disinfected estate boundaries and only allowed to talk to their disgruntled families over the gates. A garage was filled with a large quantity of beds and dressing tables which arrived by van from Tunbridge Wells and this became the men's home for three weeks. At night time the sisters arranged some improving entertainment. Carpeting was laid down in the hall and dining room of the manor so that the men could attend a recital on the gramophone of classical music. As the evening progressed the latch of the front door was heard to fall repeatedly as one by one the men crept back to their quarters.

The threat of foot and mouth receded much to everyone's relief. The herd had reached championship status and, despite its owners' extravagances being scorned by the locals, the farm had a high reputation in the county. The sisters' relationship was close and outwardly affectionate but little sign of warmth appeared between Frances and her husband. 'The Captain' was a slight, reticent man who knew little of farming and was overshadowed by his wife's dominating nature. But they were united in their pride and love of their only child. Douglas was a cheerful, friendly boy. Dark and slightly built, he was not good looking but had an earnest, deliberate way of speaking and an unassuming confidence that were immediately attractive. His parents had sent him to Eton where he was doing well, winning his house colours commendably early and proving to be a good athlete and scholar. He had decided on a diplomatic career and his parents had already reserved one of their cottages for his eventual occupation. His future looked particularly bright.

In the summer of 1927 when Douglas was 16 years old, he made plans to join the school camp at Aldershot and then to travel by train to Scotland where he would holiday with his parents at Ballachulish in the Western Highlands. He wrote to his parents from Eton to make the final arrangements, his letters full of the cricket matches in which he was representing his house. 'Darling Mummie', he wrote, 'We have got into the final of the cricket, but I rather doubt if we shall win. I have done quite well so far, touch wood, and I will tell you about it when I return .... I am longing for Scotland.' To his delight, Douglas's house won the coveted cricket cup and the summer camp was generally voted a success. On Wednesday evening of 3rd August Douglas and some school friends boarded the night sleeper at Euston where his father had reserved him a first-class compartment. In the early hours of the next morning he was found unconscious and wearing only his pyjamas on the line 40 miles from Carlisle. He was taken to the Cumberland Infirmary and died of a fractured skull on the Friday morning. His parents, who had arrived at the hospital the night before, were with him when he died.   He had never regained consciousness.

At the inquest held in Carlisle a set of mysterious circumstances were revealed. The boy had ordered tea to be brought to his compartment at 8 am at which hour the attendant reported him missing from his berth. His clothes and belongings had not been tampered with. Marks of his fingers and bare feet were discovered on the windowsill and on the gutter of the train roof. The jury brought in a verdict of 'Death from injuries accidentally received from falling from a moving train'. The Coroner remarked that Douglas had apparently deliberately climbed out of his window, but with what purpose, or under what conditions, they were left to imagine. Suicide was ruled out because he was such a cheerful boy.   The possibility of foul play was not explored.

The family returned immediately to Northease Manor where the ladies went into deepest mourning. Douglas was buried alongside his grandfather in the family grave at Mereworth in Kent;   farm workers wearing their smocks were ferried to the funeral in a taxi in order to carry the coffin.   His father walked silently across the Northease acres, while his mother withdrew into an inglenook fireplace in the manor and wept without ceasing.

The Eton obituary gave the likely cause of Douglas's death as 'sleepwalking' and this explanation was offered locally. It did not silence the inevitable rumours and speculation that followed the tragedy.   Friends trying to console the bereaved parents did not know what to say for the best. One letter of condolence sent from Kensington Palace on behalf of the boy's godmother, Princess Louise, suggested that all the finest young men were being taken for a purpose which would be revealed to the faithful in due course. Many years later when the ladies lived in Lewes, they confided to some close friends that the boy had died as a result of horseplay with the other Eton boys on the train. If this was so, were the members of the jury at the inquest, who were taken to see the compartment in the train, persuaded to hush the matter up? Whatever the truth, Douglas's death had a profound effect on the family. Frances and her husband, united only in their love for their son, grew even further apart. They lost interest in the estate which, due to their extravagance, was now in financial difficulties. They decided to give up farming and sell out. From then on the sisters determined to throw themselves into the arts to help assuage their loss.

Details of the next ten years are sketchy but it is known that the family moved to Pembrokeshire where they rented Manorbier Castle. Caroline, who had already exhibited her paintings in London, Paris and Rome, studied sculpture in London with John Skeaping in a group with, improbably, Agatha Christie. In the 1930s she had 'one-man' exhibitions of both paintings and sculpture at the Lefevre and Leicester Galleries in London. During these years she alternated between Pembrokeshire and a studio at 77 Bedford Gardens which housed a coterie of other artists. Frances became a founder member of the Contemporary Arts Society for Wales. A formidable organiser, she advised on the purchase of works of art by contemporary artists not solely from Wales and worked closely with Augustus John, Ceri Richards, Cedric Morris and other artists in the principality. It was Cedric Morris who in 1935 painted two revealing portraits of the ladies, one entitled *The Sisters* and the other of Frances alone. Morris much disliked the English class system and took to referring to the joint portrait as 'The English Upper Classes'. Both portraits were for him an experimental exercise in colour with which he was well pleased but the ladies took offence at the pictures and ceased all further communication.

✳

During the War

In 1939 Edwin Byng-Stamper died and the sisters decided to return to Sussex, open Miller's Gallery and devote their lives to developing a regional centre of the arts. They used their many influential friends shamelessly in their crusade and enlisted the support of the critics Raymond Mortimer, Desmond MacCarthy and Joe Ackerley in publicising the gallery. Clive and Vanessa Bell and Duncan Grant at nearby Charleston were closely involved in the venture, as was their next-door neighbour at Tilton, Maynard Keynes. He had become Chairman of CEMA, the Council for the Encouragement of Music and the Arts, (forerunner of The Arts Council), and ensured that Miller's received the cream of the exhibitions touring the country under the 'Art for the People' scheme.

The ladies' manners were exquisite and they achieved their objectives by means of charming notes, persuasive telephone calls and invitations to tea.

Angelica Garnett recalls them as reminding her of Mrs Gaskell's novel *Cranford*, with all the hesitations, reservations and conventionalities of spinsters. They served tea in the most delicate china cups, and her mother, Vanessa Bell, considered her own home-made earthenware not quite up-to-scratch when the ladies visited Charleston. These visits were not frequent for Vanessa Bell preferred them at second remove. She treated them with kid gloves but was irritated by their pretensions, pointing out tartly that they could not even claim an 'honourable' between them. She had no time for such snobberies, while being comfortably clear about her own aristocratic connections. The sisters, too, preferred to have Duncan Grant all to themselves. He enchanted them with his beautiful manners and his capacity of showing a delicate, attentive affection which never went beyond certain unspoken but well defined limits. For his part, Duncan Grant was both amused and touched by the two women, genuinely fond of them and admiring of their tenacity. He wrote at the time: 'Mrs Byng-Stamper and her sister Miss Lucas do their work without the help of any Committee whatever. No doubt they ask advice of those from whom they wish it, but there results no compromise, arising from a too great variety of taste or ideas. For good or for ill, on questions of Art, therefore, Miller's glories in the unhampered expression of its own beliefs.' His diaries show how closely involved he was with the Miller's enterprise, weeks at a time being taken up with helping the sisters arrange and hang the exhibitions. Their close relationship caused some amusement at Charleston, Maynard Keynes commenting that Duncan would have to marry the ladies - both of them.

The first exhibition of modern French and English paintings (including works by Cézanne, Matisse, Pissarro, Augustus John and Sickert) was to be opened by Sir Kenneth Clark, Director of the National Gallery and another influential friend of the Charlestonians. At the last moment, urgent war matters delayed him and a local historian was rustled up as a replacement. As he read out an apologetic letter from Kenneth Clark, the ominous sound of German bombers on their way to London was heard overhead. Despite this inauspicious start, the exhibition was a tremendous success and within a short time Miller's Gallery had gained a considerable reputation with members being recruited to subscribe between one and five shillings annually. Clive Bell reported to Frances Partridge: 'I suppose you know that Lewes (Miller's) is now become one of the cultural centres of Europe. The two indefatigable ladies ... are chiefly responsible, but Duncan must bear his share. There is said to be bitter jealousy in Brighton. One little set-back there was, when a gouache by Miró was left standing face outward beside a car and a mongrel lifted his leg against it. The picture was of course insured, but it is feared that if the story gets about owners may be less willing to lend; on the other hand, owners of Mirós may be more willing.'

One exhibition of particular note was the fine show of sculpture in 1942 including works by Rodin, Maillol, Degas, Epstein, Moore and Hepworth. Bishop Bell of

Chichester opened the exhibition and expressed his gratitude to the organisers for 'helping to keep the lamp of art burning in these war-driven days'. Duncan Grant was persuaded to write a preface to the catalogue, which, he wrote to his mother, was not easy as he knew nothing of the subject. Several of the bronzes were lent by Kenneth Clark who also gave much practical support. Later in the year he opened an exhibition of French and English watercolours and drawings with fine nudes by Degas and Ingres lent by Maynard Keynes and works by Renoir and Toulouse-Lautrec lent by W Rees Jeffrey from his notable collection in Sussex. The county was then, as now, rich in artists and collectors but the ladies undoubtedly achieved something of a scoop when Ernest Duveen, the art dealer and collector, agreed to lend them his magnificent collection of European paintings. For two weeks Miller's was hung with paintings by Picasso, Bonnard, Modigliani, Chagall, Derain, Segonzac, Utrillo, Sickert and Stanley Spencer.

A CEMA exhibition of special local interest was held in 1941 called '1000 Years of Lewes'. Clive Bell wrote the catalogue preface and drew attention to the 'claims of the county town to fame and notoriety, quite apart from 1066 and the Battle of Lewes. Visitors are reminded that Lewes Priory was the oldest daughter of Cluny and that Lewes played a part in shaping the future of the Sackvilles, the Pelhams and the great Duke of Newcastle, and also of the not less well-known Tom Paine ... But the Bonfire Clubs, though we do ourselves the honour of illustrating their activities need no memorial: they have seen to it that they, like the event they commemorate, shall never be forgot.' The exhibition, with exhibits dating from the 11th Century, included from the ancient Lewes Priory its Foundation Charter, beautifully painted mediaeval tiles and a 13th century stone head found at the bottom of a stream. From the 16th and 17th centuries there were fine portraits, including one described by Duncan Grant as 'a curious and fascinating portrait of Thomas Sackville, the lst Earl of Dorset'. Other exhibits included an 18th century engraving of Tom Paine, a pen and ink drawing of Lewes by John Byng, Baxter prints, playbills, Bonfire posters, Lewes race cards and some of the famous collection of Edward Reeves 19th century photographs. The exhibition was not surprisingly extremely popular.

While Miller's was primarily a gallery, the other arts were not neglected. Music and dance recitals were a regular feature, a song recital by Peter Pears and a ballet evening with Lydia Lopokova, wife of Maynard Keynes, receiving enthusiastic receptions. As lack of space restricted the size of audiences, the ladies persuaded John Christie to open up Glyndebourne Opera House which had closed at the beginning of the war. In October 1941, a week or so after nine bombs fell on Lewes, music lovers were able to forget the ugliness of war at the first concert by the Dartington Hall Music Group under the direction of Hans Oppenheim. Many of the audience had walked the miles to Glyndebourne because of petrol restrictions. Several more concerts were given there, one featuring the oboist Leon Goossens to an 'overflowing' opera house.

In the field of drama the sisters arranged play readings and mounted an exhibition titled 'The Artist Plans' with a model of a theatre, art gallery, cinema and restaurant. Duncan Grant and Vanessa Bell decorated the theatre while a range of artists including Ivon Hitchens submitted designs for decor and Ethel Mairet produced hand-woven fabrics. For film buffs the Academy Cinema sent a selection of films to be shown locally. These included a film the sisters had themselves made in 1939, *The Caves of Perigord,* on the subject of the prehistoric cave paintings of the region, with specially commissioned incidental music. Photography was also represented by an exhibition 'The Eye of the Camera' to which Vanessa Bell lent her collection of photographs by her great-aunt Julia Cameron.

The lectures featured an enterprising range of speakers and topics. Kenneth Clark spoke on drawing, Herbert Marshall discussed Shakespeare on the Soviet stage, J T Shepherd talked about Homer and Quentin Bell brought his collection of dress fashion illustrations. E M Forster lectured on literature between the wars, Clive Bell writing to Frances Partridge: 'Morgan was here for the weekend and gave an admirable discourse to the people of Miller's - very intelligent, very amusing and profoundly depressing: it pleased the artists and annoyed the politicians - which is just as it should be.' Desmond MacCarthy chose Ibsen as his subject and was asked afterwards by Duncan Grant if he would put it into print. He refused, writing that to publish a lecture was to kill it and that he intended to make money out of the same lecture for years to come. Leonard Woolf rode over on his bicycle from Rodmell and gave an enjoyably gloomy exposé of 'The Trade of Literature'. He offered little comfort to anyone contemplating being a writer, publisher or bookseller; integrity in the book trade, he suggested, was hard to find. In 1945 Janie Bussy, the French painter, came to stay at Charleston and talked at Miller's on life in occupied France. The ladies, who had travelled and studied extensively in France, were staunch Francophiles. As they affected unnecessary French pronunciations and claimed, untruthfully, that they spoke the language fluently, the Charlestonians joked that it was the sisters who had liberated France single-handed.

While the gallery was an undoubted artistic triumph, the sisters were not appreciated by everyone in the town. They were often laughed at behind their backs and they attracted a number of nicknames, 'The Ladies of Miller's' being the most polite. Frances was sometimes referred to unkindly as 'Mrs Byng-Horser' because of her unfortunate resemblance to that animal. One epithet, 'The Geese Women', derived from their inseparability and their manner of walking up and down the High Street. Frances walked bent from the waist, her left hand extended with fingers pointing forward. She frequently looked back at her sister who shuffled along behind. Both wore the vague myopic look of those deeply preoccupied by the mysteries of high art. Apart from their disconcerting plainness - Clive Bell described them as 'two uglies moulded on one stem' - their clothes were a shock to conservative Lewes. Caroline was especially 'arty', wearing long Ethel Mairet hand-woven drapes and colourful turbans. They insisted on the best, regularly spending their food coupons at Fortnum and Masons. Clive Bell remarked to Frances Partridge: 'the indefatigable ladies of Miller's ... think about nothing but food and the fine arts, which is very comfortable.' Their extravagance and generosity to their friends was, however, combined with penny-pinching and tardiness in paying their bills. When Frances's old Dior dresses wore out, a local seamstress was employed to make copies and sew in the original labels. Appearances had at all times to be maintained. It is difficult in these egalitarian days to appreciate the strict adherence to the social niceties that prevailed in the town at this time. An acquaintance of the ladies recalled her own feeling of guilt when as a girl she cycled past a policeman without wearing a hat. Her father, a solicitor and a chapelgoer, would not have been acknowledged in the street by a fellow professional who was a churchgoer and one rung up on the social ladder. A young woman who wished to rent one of the ladies' properties had her letter ignored because she lived in the Pells area of the town, which they considered to be undesirable. Once the sisters discovered that she had studied at The Slade School of Art, however, they were all charm and graciously granted her request. People and places were either 'in' or 'out'. The late Clifford Musgrave, then Director of the Brighton Pavilion, Art Gallery and Museums, wrote in his memoirs: 'With Frances and Caroline one was often 'out' on one day and 'in' on another.' On one occasion when he had incurred their disapproval, a mutual friend protested to the ladies: "'But you told me that you thought Clifford Musgrave was a genius?" "In moderation, in moderation", was Frances' reply.' Soon after, the genius in moderation was once more restored to favour.

The ladies by now owned a good many properties in the town. They often bought up period buildings that were in danger of falling down but then did little to preserve them. They were bad landlords insisting on rent being paid on the dot but ignoring tenants' pleas to do something about the poor state of the houses. A small terraced house backing on to Miller's was purchased to house the sisters' comprehensive collection of art books which were then lent out to suitable readers. One large Lewes building, The Tabernacle, a little used Congregational chapel at the bottom of the town, was thought by the ladies to be the ideal venue for a school of dramatic art. Maynard Keynes and the actor and director Michel St Denis were involved in the project and negotiations between the ladies and the church committee started in 1939. The sisters were mean bargainers, as Leonard Woolf found when trying to buy a small piece of land adjoining his garden from the Northease estate years earlier, but eventually it seemed that their offer of £3,500 would be accepted and imaginative plans were drawn up for its conversion into a theatre. Seats for 250 people were to be allocated downstairs with the option of additional seating or a picture exhibition down one aisle. The gallery was to be reserved for children's benches and a cafe was proposed. Especial care was to be taken over the preservation of the organ, pews, pulpit and stained glass windows. In 1942 the committee suddenly decided that the future was unpredictable and that the building might be worth more after the war. They withdrew the chapel from the market. Ten years or so later The Tabernacle was demolished and this interesting early 19th century building was replaced by an ugly modern store.

Eleven months after the first opening of the gallery, Miller's sent a report to all its members, of whom there were now eight hundred. In that short time it had held four major exhibitions, five lectures, three concerts (both at Miller's and Glyndebourne) and a film show. The sisters' energies were formidable. In 1942 they purchased yet another property, a studio in East Street, Lewes, and started up a painting school with Caroline, Vanessa Bell and Duncan Grant as teachers. Life classes were held on three days a week and on other days classes were held in design, composition and mural painting. Exhibitions were also given of students' work.

On November 5th 1945 the Bonfire Societies renewed the famous festivities that had been suspended during the war. The event, which is generally noisy and boisterous, was moving and impressive as the long procession marched with its flaming torches through the streets of Lewes in complete silence. The Charlestonians and Raymond Mortimer had supper with the ladies in the gallery.

Clive Bell commented to Frances Partridge: ' ... excellent Burgundy was produced - God knows how'. The gallery was no longer needed for CEMA exhibitions as they had come to an end, but at an age when retirement might have seemed desirable, the sisters had yet another idea as to where to channel their artistic energies.

✳

After the War

The ladies' new and imaginative venture was to turn their attention to lithography and set up the Miller's Press. Lithography in Britain had at that time been much neglected partly because it was regarded as an esoteric craft but also because of the difficulties of the process. Artists had no alternative but to draw their designs on to the stones in reverse in the bustle of a lithographic workshop. Colour printing had been in the main reserved for reproductions of popular paintings and the potential of original colour lithography had not been fully realised.

The ladies aimed to encourage British artists to become 'peintres graveurs' as in France and to produce not only black and white and colour lithographs but also monotypes and aquatints. In 1945 CEMA had sent Miller's a lithographic exhibition mainly featuring European artists. To these works the ladies had added their own first publication - a portfolio of lithographs, hand-pulled and on hand-made paper, by Caroline

Lucas, H E du Plessis, Vanessa Bell and Duncan Grant. In these lithographs the influence of French painting and printmaking is noticeable, giving a satisfying unity to the set. Copies were immediately purchased by several galleries including the Victoria and Albert Museum, while a review in The Listener praised 'the enterprising art centre' for its first essay in publishing. Encouraged by this reception, the ladies joined forces with the Redfern Gallery in London, then as now champions of lithography, and set up The Society of London Painter-Printers. The sisters resourcefully overcame artists' resistance to the process of lithography by re-introducing the 19th century method of using transfer papers so that artists could create designs in their own studios. These designs were at first sent to the Chiswick Press for printing but as the press could not cope with the volume of work, the ladies also distributed drawings to the master printer, Louis Ravel, in Paris. Both methods have their own distinctive style, the Chiswick work displaying an attractive gaiety and lightness while the French printing produces a velvety depth in the blacks and a richness in the colours. The sisters also used their own press at Miller's, paying scrupulous attention to the quality of paper and inks and to the standard of press work. Annual exhibitions were given at the Redfern Gallery and the work disseminated by the British Council and the Arts Council to the Commonwealth and the Continent.

Miller's commissioned many of the lithographs direct, paying the artists at source and encouraged work by an astonishing range of artists. In the first exhibition 171 entries were listed alphabetically from Jankel Adler to Bryan Wynter and included prints by William Scott, Ceri Richards, Matthew Smith, Graham Sutherland, Paul Nash and John Piper. Clive Bell wrote an introduction to the catalogue in which he enthused: 'Here is an admirable Project, and, as one might have guessed, Miller's is at the bottom of it. To Miller's, a Society created and ruled by the white but surprisingly firm hands of two ladies ... lovers of beauty are once again in debt.' He referred to 'the fine and surprising range of contemporary British artists, some of whom are already famous, some of whom are generally reckoned promising, but of whom very few twelve months ago had serious thoughts of practising this delightful craft.'

In 1946 Caroline Lucas produced her own portfolio of six lithographs of Lewes and Brighton in which she commemorated the tour into Sussex in 1788 by her ancestor John Byng, author of *The Torrington Diaries.* These diaries in 24 volumes were found in the 1930s scattered around the country in libraries and second-hand book shops, and are written in a clear, scholarly hand. Pasted on almost every page are contemporary prints of the places he visited, maps, advertisements, newspaper cuttings and bills from the inns he had stayed at. They achieve a wonderful intimacy. The Honourable John Byng, later to become the Fifth Viscount, had been a Lieutenant-Colonel in the Foot Guards and then a Civil Servant and Commissioner of Stamps. He summed up his life laconically:-

'His early days were spent in Camps
His latter days were passed at Stamps.'

Every year he escaped from his unfaithful invalid
wife and 13 children to tour on horseback through
England. Unlike his great-great-granddaughters, he
was entirely free from snobbishness, and when he
visited famous houses did so as an ordinary tourist. He
was accompanied by a friend on foot, 'the famous
pedestrian Mr D'. They sent their luggage on in
advance and attempted to meet up each evening. 'I
abound with curiosity', he said, 'or else I should stay in
London'. A compassionate but critical traveller, he
grumbled his way through Kent, into Sussex and back
through Surrey to London. He described Rye as
smelling of fish and punch, but when Mr D persuaded
him to move on from their hostelry to Winchelsea, he
was not pleased, for he wrote that you should 'never
quarrel with your bread and butter'. Nor did he think
much of Brighton which was 'in a fashionable, unhappy
bustle with such a harpy set of painted harlots as to
appear to me as bad as Bond Street in the Spring'. On
August 2nd, he arrived in Lewes and stayed at the
White Hart where he considered the only good thing
was some brill fish. He walked up to the castle with its
gateway 'blocked up by houses' and then to St John's
churchyard where he was fascinated to find an
inscription on a coffin lid to a Danish warrior.
'Antiquity can go no further back', he wrote. Rain
forced him to shelter in a poor woman's cottage near

the Priory ruins. He was deeply aware of the miseries of the poor and commented: 'All the rich and gay World, huddled together in London, on Turkey carpets before Register Stoves, can but little conceive The Pangs of Poverty'. That evening his wife 'Mrs B' arrived with their son Henry who was to be placed at a Lewes school ('seemingly very fit for little Fellows'). Later that night their bedroom door was 'forced upon by Drunkards which alarm'd Mrs B exceedingly'. His final comment on the Lewes hostelries was: 'There cannot be an Inn of a worse description than is this White Hart and the Star looks as badly'. Over one hundred and fifty years later the ladies made up for his comments by regularly entertaining the Charlestonians to lunch at the White Hart in Lewes. Caroline's commemorative portfolio consisted of two lithographs of Lewes town, two of Brighton sea front and an 18th century map of each place, with an accompanying description of the diaries and appropriate excerpts. When drawing the Brighton scenes, she insisted on hiring a hotel bedroom on the sea front for the purpose.

In 1946 the ladies decided to use one of their Lewes properties for an unusual artistic experiment. Westgate House, conveniently close to Millers, is a fine 18th century town house distinguished by having part of the old town wall in its fabric. They offered the house for use by Langford Grove, a progressive girls' boarding school at Barcombe Mills, near Lewes, run by Mrs Curtis. Mrs Elizabeth Curtis, a well-connected and redoubtable woman of Irish descent, ran the school on unorthodox and permissive educational lines, with

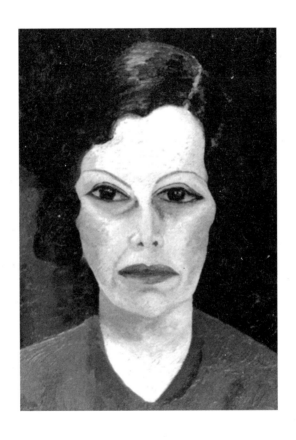

Cedric Morris *The Sisters* 1935 Detail of Caroline

particular emphasis on the arts. Girls, as Angelica Garnett discovered when a pupil some years earlier, could give up any subject they found tiresome, and the sciences were not taught at all. Amongst the staff was Marjorie Strachey, who delighted the girls by teaching English and history in a cloud of tobacco smoke and surrounded by detective novels. Mrs Curtis was an inspirational headmistress with an inexhaustible fund of enthusiasm - girls would be roused from their beds to witness a particularly spectacular sunrise or suddenly taken to a play or exhibition if the reviews were favourable. The ladies were impressed by Mrs Curtis's tall elegance, her aristocratic manner and her sensitivity to the visual arts. She collected modern pictures and was the first private collector to buy paintings by Frances Hodgkins, who often stayed at the school. The sisters took a keen interest in the school and Caroline gave painting instruction to the girls.

It was decided that half-a-dozen particularly gifted girls would be moved to Westgate House where they would receive special instruction from Caroline on painting, pottery and sculpture. She walked her pupils up the road to learn the mechanics of lithography on the Miller's lithographic press. Caroline was not a good teacher, her attempts to be 'one of the girls' by hinting at the numerous lovers she had had fell rather flat. The girls laughed at her blowsy appearance, her large bosom and her old-fashioned use of lace, scarves and long beads. The staff at the house were singularly unsuitable for looking after their charges. The cook was a sinister peroxide blonde who refused to cook vegetarian dishes for one of the girls, who therefore went hungry. The housekeeper, a German woman, had frequent fainting fits on the stairs and had to be dragged up to her attic bedroom. After Hermann Goering committed suicide to escape execution, she kept shouting disconcertingly at the girls 'We will win in the end!' Classes were even less structured than at Langford Grove as the pupils, relishing their new-found freedom, escaped lengthily into the town. That year on November 5th the girls were keen to go to the outskirts of the town to see one of the Bonfire Society's celebrations. They ignored the staff's express instructions not to go and stayed till after midnight. The experiment was abandoned after a year.

The following year Westgate House was again pressed into service for the arts with rather more fruitful results. Two artists who created many lithographs for the Miller's Press were the Scottish painters, Colquhoun and MacBryde. In 1941 'the Roberts', as they were known, moved into 77 Bedford Gardens, the former home of Caroline Lucas. Through mutual friends such as Dylan Thomas, Jankel Adler and John Minton, the ladies met Colquhoun and MacBryde and Frances was impressed by their work. Their paintings had caught the imagination of a post-war audience with their emphatic imagery and emotional appeal. While MacBryde was the more adventurous with colour, Colquhoun's Celtic-inspired tragic vision was of a haunting originality. In 1947 the Roberts were thrown out of their studio by their landlord for 'drunken orgies' and were promptly offered a home by the ladies. They installed the artists in Westgate House and gave them not only encouragement but financial support. It is entertaining to consider the exquisite, well-bred sisters taking under their wing this pair of hard-living, hard-drinking homosexuals. It was a particularly successful liaison for under these congenial conditions Colquhoun and MacBryde produced some of their finest work. Colquhoun was particularly productive, painting a series of women with goats and a set of colour lithographs for 'Poems of Sleep and Dream' published by Frederick Muller. Both artists were also commissioned by Léonide Massine to create the costumes and decor for a Scottish ballet, 'Donald of the Burthens'. These colourful and vigorous designs depict a pre-tartan Scotland where the feeling of locality is conveyed by the use of Celtic symbol and ornament. The ballet was eventually produced in 1951 at Covent Garden with some success, it being the first time bagpipes had been heard at the opera house. When these designs were later exhibited at the Redfern Gallery, Colin Anderson wrote: 'From the first it had been agreed that a course must be steered to avoid either the Follies Bergère 'style écossaise' with its kilted panties of tartan moiré and peeps of lace, or the aggressive Dagenham Girl Piper effect, with its travesty of male dress. Heather, thistles and haggis were also to be avoided and this has been achieved without in the least sacrificing the feeling of the locality, although these are the costumes of a Scotland still Celtic.'

The first year of the Roberts' stay, some of the girls who had been involved in the ill-fated artistic experiment of the previous year, returned to Lewes on Bonfire Night to watch the festivities and visit their former lodgings. At Westgate House they saw an alarming number of men congregating, but were welcomed by Colquhoun with the words: 'Have no fear for your virginity, girls - step right in.' Later, MacBryde expansively offered one of the girls a sheaf of lithographs, to be told reprovingly by Colquhoun that he would regret it in the morning.

In 1949 George Barker, the poet and friends of the Roberts, visited Lewes and asked Colquhoun to illustrate his proposed book on the Italian scene for John Lehmann. The Miller's Press backed this commission with one of its own for a series of lithographs on the same theme. The Roberts left for Italy later in the year to fulfil these commissions and also to see the puppet plays at Modena. In the event the book never materialised but the Miller's Press lithographs were completed and the puppet plays stimulated a further series of paintings and prints. It was after their return from Italy that misfortune struck the artists in the death of Duncan Macdonald, director of the Lefevre Gallery, who had long been their friend and active supporter. This was a severe blow to the artists who decided to move to Essex to live with George Barker and his family. From this point, however, both the private lives and the output of the Roberts gradually deteriorated, although Frances continued to be a loyal collector of their work.

Apart from its lithographic activities, the Miller's Press experimented in publishing a book on the ancient frescoes of the Sussex churches at Hardham and Clayton. These fine 13th century murals were photographed by Helmut Gernsheim with Caroline providing tracings of the original designs. The Charlestonians were closely involved with the project, Clive Bell contributing a long introductory essay and Duncan Grant accompanying the ladies on their visits to the churches where, to Vanessa Bell's entertainment, Caroline inadvertently stepped on a bat.

In 1946 the gallery was once more put to use to house an exhibition. The Arts Council (which had replaced CEMA) sponsored 'Art and Utility', an exhibition of the textiles, furniture and pottery made in the Omega Workshops between 1913-18 under the direction of Roger Fry. The Omega items displayed a combination of artistic design with the production of everyday household needs. The exhibition so revived Vanessa Bell's and Duncan Grant's interest in decorative work that for a time they seriously considered reviving the Omega. The exhibition was opened by Leigh Ashton, director of the Victoria & Albert Museum, who was introduced by Clive Bell. Later Clive Bell wrote that 'dear old Leigh' was to be likened to a whim of Edward Lear's:-

'There was an old man with no legs
Who was made of a couple of eggs.'

The next year Miller's took the initiative in forming a committee to raise a fund to preserve and maintain the then disgracefully neglected remains of the ancient

Lewes Priory, and produced an attractive illustrated pamphlet to launch a national appeal. Apart from the ladies, leading historians and archaeologists were induced to join the committee whose aim was to assist the Borough Council, who had bought them in 1945, to care for the ruins. The Council, however, had other ideas. Councillors expressed the worrying thought that if the ruins were restored, they would have to maintain them, one saying: 'I do not think we should be responsible for spending any sum of money on a thing which cannot do the present generation much good.' Yet another said craftily that the Council should not spend a lot of money on the ruins, but only take a great interest in them. The appeal totalled £166 5s 7d, although the Pilgrim Trust was persuaded to make a grant of £1,500 over 3 years. It appears that, for once, the ladies had met their match.

In the mid-1950s, the ladies found their lithographic activities too taxing and the Miller's Press was disbanded. A final exhibition entitled 'Contemporary British Lithographs published by Miller's of Lewes' was given by the Arts Council in 1954 with a foreword by Philip James in which he described the collection as 'an incentive and a yardstick for those interested in the graphic arts'.

In 1957 the sisters suggested and organised an exhibition with Clifford Musgrave on 'The Influence of Wales in Painting', held in the Brighton Pavilion Art Gallery. They gave considerable help in selecting and securing the loan of many of the pictures from their Welsh artist friends and from the Contemporary Arts

Society of Wales which Frances had helped found in the 1930s. The exhibition was also not just concerned with its native artists but with the impact of the spirit and scenery of the land of Wales upon artists from elsewhere in the British Isles. Paintings included works by Augustus and Gwen John, Graham Sutherland, Kyffin Williams, John Piper, Ceri Richards, Henry Lamb, Patricia Preece, JMWTurner, JDInnes, Colquhoun and MacBryde and Caroline herself. The exhibition was very successful and visited by thousands of people. But afterwards the enthusiasm of the ladies for promoting the arts seemed to wane. They were, at last, beginning to feel their age.

In the early 1960s the ladies became very frail and moved next door to Shelley's Hotel where they both charmed and terrorised the staff and residents. They insisted on the best suite with bathroom, despite the fact that, regrettably, they never used the bath. They were not easy guests, sticking an imperious arm out to stop a heavily laden waitress dead in her tracks and banging with their walking sticks on the bedroom floor to summon assistance. They bent over their soup like skeletons but were canny enough to drink some wine, complain about it and ask for the carafe to be refilled. In December 1967 Caroline died at the age of 81, and a distraught Frances, who had always assumed she would die first, asked for her will to be changed at eleven o'clock that night. A few months later, unwilling to continue without her inseparable companion, she too died. Both ladies to the end refused to give their correct ages.

Today there remains little evidence of the sisters' life and aspirations. It had been hoped that the ladies' paintings, lithographs and papers would pass on their deaths to the University of Sussex. For years the sisters had hinted broadly to the then Vice-Chancellor, now Lord Briggs of Lewes, that they would leave their collection with an endowment to the University. During charming conversations over lengthy lunches, they asked for and received the benefit of his advice on this and many other matters. Apart from the pleasure of their company, he received nothing in return. The loss to the University and to the county was considerable for in the event the gallery was demolished, their possessions were split up and most of their correspondence destroyed. While a good many people had reason to be grateful to them for their wartime activities, their dream of creating a centre of regional art was short lived, for as Clive Bell feared: 'perhaps in a country so small as Britain, and in modern conditions, decentralisation is past praying for.' Their influence on the revival of post-war lithography should not, however, be underestimated and their patronage enabled many a struggling artist to survive. Memories of these extraordinary women are still strong but will in time inevitably fade. This small book is an attempt to pay a permanent tribute to two enterprising and indomitable patrons of the arts - the ladies of Miller's.

✳✳

Note on Sources

Nearly all the papers left relating to the Ladies are in private hands. A few were donated to The Sussex Archaeological Society and can be seen at the East Sussex Records Office, Lewes, under reference SAS ACC 1299.

Information on the sisters' art and lithography exhibitions and local activities was obtained by scanning 40 or so years of local newspapers, held on microfilm at the East Sussex Records Office, Lewes, and the Brighton Reference Library. The archives of The Listener and The New Statesman were consulted for specific reviews. Further information was found from viewing Duncan Grant's diaries and Clive Bell's letters, both unpublished.

'A Tour Into Sussex' from *The Torrington Diaries* is printed in The Sussex County Magazine Vol. 7, and can be borrowed from the Sussex Room of the East Sussex County Library, Lewes. A copy of the original diary can be viewed in the Brighton Reference Library under reference S9.

✳

The cover illustration showing Lewes High Street is taken from a "Vignette Letter Card" date and origin unknown.